DAYLIGHT

Also by Elaine Feinstein from Carcanet

Selected Poems

ELAINE FEINSTEIN

DAYLIGHT

CARCANET

First published in 1997 by
Carcanet Press Limited
4th Floor, Conavon Court
12-16 Blackfriars Street
Manchester M3 5BQ

A CIP catalogue record for this book
is available from the British Library
ISBN 1 85754 291 6

The publisher acknowledges financial assistance
from the Arts Council of England

Set in 10pt Palatino by Bryan Williamson, Frome
Printed and bound in England by SRP Ltd, Exeter

For Arnold

Acknowledgements

Some of these poems have appeared in: *The Times Literary Supplement, Poetry Review, New Statesman, Spectator, London Review of Books, Poetry Nation Review, London Quarterly* and *Soundings*.

Contents

Homesickness

In Memory of Maria Fadeyeva Enzensberger

Yesterday I found a postcard with your scrawl:
'Darling, we are all horses, how is it
you haven't learned that yet?' And at once
your high-boned, white face rose
beside me like a reproach

as if I had begun to forget the wildness
in the gutturals of your laugh, and
the loneliness of *tosca po rodine*
in the frozen sea of your eyes. But I have not.
You were always my Russia:

the voice of Marina's poetry. We saw you last
in a Moscow of brown streets, puddles, and
people queuing for ice cream: an autumn of anomalies,
women turning back tanks, in St Petersburg
there were teenage boys playing *Deutschland uber alles.*

Your mother, the poet Aliger, brought us into
Sologub's yellow mansion where Ivan found himself
in his underpants and writers fix their *dachas*:
Bulgakov would have enjoyed the chicken livers in coriander.
That day you were shaking with the euphoria

of street victory, as if you had come home
after the bleakness that took you into
Highgate hospital. 'I have been so *frightened,*'
you whispered to me there and I had no answer,
any more than at your table in the Cambridge fens

rich with forest mushrooms, peppers and white cheese,
when you struck the glass to command some speech
of love and closeness, and we all failed you. In London
you found another silence, and now we're only left with
a little honey and sun from Mandelstam's dead bees.

Little Venice

For David

Sunlight on the canal, seagulls and a few boats
low in the water: this street is no longer
your territory but as I drive through,
the cool remembered glitter conjures you:
that note of surprise in your voice
as you tell me of some disaster, your
shoulders shaking in those soft blue
Hemingway roll necks. It was your charm
to have the world become a Truffaut film,
or a Brassens song, in the shared laughter.

'Too clever for your own good,' your Cambridge tutor
said, annoyed to have you bypass steady work
in phrasing essays with a casual wit.
I can't remember who it was you hit,
or why the story passed into your legend,
with Paris, Vietnam, and those Insight bylines
which were a part of the same dangerous glamour,
though underneath you were
always lonely in a childhood anger
women never quite escaped.

You startled me on the telephone yesterday
speaking of a dead friend: *'We both loved you.*
You must have known that.' What I knew
was the way we lived in one another's
imagination, rather as people in the novels
of Malcolm Lowry. Closer companions
coped with daily behaviour. All the same,
your words reached through an unhappy
morning to restore my stamina.

Tony

It was February in Provence and the local market
sold goats' cheese wrapped in chestnut leaves and
thick, painted pottery. The stalls of dark check shirts
were the kind you used to wear, and we began to see you:
burly, bearded, handsome as Holbein's Wyatt,
looking into the eyes of a girl or
jumping up from the brasserie table
to buy truffles from a street vendor.

We stayed with our children like gypsies in a barn
of your wife's family house near Aix, and you fed us
beef *daube*, thrush pâté and wine. Long ago
we sat through the night as a threesome writing
those film reviews I always drove to Heffers
in the early rainlight of a Cambridge morning. We still own
the pearwood Dolmetsch bought at your urging,
and copies of that magazine you and I ran together

which the police came to investigate after
a delivery of *Naked Lunch* from Olympia.
For a few years, you moved whenever we did,
from Adams Road to Sherlock, then De Freville
where the printer we owed money lived next door.
You wrote your first book for three hours a day
and then felt restless, since your body liked
to use its energies and you could lift a car.

Your hair was thick and brown
even in York District Hospital where you murmured
'I'm not dying, am I?' and described
the wild animals calmed with a click in your throat.
We guessed you could withstand a February *mistral*
that gets under the clothes so bitterly down here
more easily than we can, being younger
and more robust though, strangely, no longer alive.

Postcard from the Sporades

You know so much about islands.
Here we are woken by cocks and donkeys.
Village women pick thyme and fennel
below our stone terrace: the air
is heavy with a sweet-smelling citrus.

In Waterstones, I watched you listening
to an Irish Poet, your mouth invisible,
the glamour of sadness in your bearing: a
scholar Garbo. We are reading your book now,
here on an island of shepherds and pirates.

Insomnia

The moon woke me, the pocked and chalky moon
that floods the garden with its silvery blue

and cuts the shadow of one leafy branch across
this bed of ours as if on to bright snow.

The sky is empty. Street lights and stars
are all extinguished. Still the moon flows in,

drowning old landmarks in a magic lake,
the chilly waters lapping at my pillow,

their spell relentless as this cold
unhappiness in which I lie awake.

Eclipse

On both sides of the gardens the tall
houses have put out their lights.
Now the cypress is blue and furry,
night creatures move quietly in the long grass,
and, as if in the ages before electricity,

the moon is a white lantern over the birch trees.
Grandchildren, indulged after the Passover seder,
have stopped using the mouse on my apple mac
to stare through the window at the luminous ball
like primitive people in a world of miracles.

This year, Katriona read the questions from the Haggadah;
Lara knew the ancient stories. Now three generations
sit together, imagining ourselves on the globe
of the earth, and trying to believe it is our own
brown shadow moving over the moon.

Izzy's Daughter

'You must be Izzy's daughter,' they said.
I was a liquid, black stare. An olive face.

'So thin. Doesn't she eat? She reads too much.'
My teasing, brawny aunts upset my mother.

I wanted to be as reckless as a man,
to dive through rough, grey waves on Southport sands,

and shake the salt out of my hair as he did.
Instead, I shivered, blue with cold, on the shore.

But I was Maggie Tulliver, proud of my cleverness,
when the whole family listened to my stories.

He listened, too; troubled, his lips moving,
and dog-brown eyes following every word.

'Where does it all come from?' they marvelled at me.
My timid mother smiled from her quiet corner.

A Glass of Wine

For Emma

In your dream, T.S. Eliot and a chestnut stallion
were being bundled into a taxi, the Old Possum
spectacled, a little furtive, the glowing animal
submissive, both dismissed together
as if from your own life. A fiction,

old friend: your spirit is the living stuff
of poetry. That first winter in Wiltshire,
when the frosty leaves crackled under
our feet, we walked beneath black trees
talking of magic and insanity,

and many times since then you've conjured
poems from sad thoughts, and with your laughter
taught me the way to shrink snubs and disasters
into absurdity, with the black wit
once labelled melancholy 'male as cricket'.

Some people shed friendships as they age
and become the family they thought they'd left behind
(stetl traders in my case, as for yours
the fashionable world came through your doors)
but we are speaking now of heart and mind;

I love your Scottish stride and sailing carriage,
yet if we lift a glass of wine at 192,
it is the inner fire still burns in you
I see and quietly salute:
indomitable wildness.

The Convalescent

A painting by Gwen John

'I may be timid, but I am never humble,' she said.
The girl she paints is alone in a cane chair.

Her blue dress gives no hint of the body beneath,
the pinks and browns on the lids of her eyes

are those of the cup and teapot. In this space,
the gaze of a lover has no importance.

The artist was often ill; she neglected herself.
Like her sitter, she was young and much too thin

when Rodin seduced her by candlelight that
first day as his model. He found it hard thereafter

to match her passion. 'Stars in the sky console me,'
she wrote, and the energy of lust went into her work.

This is her painting of another woman. It signals
a recovery from more than influenza.

Lazarus' Sister

On hot nights now, in the smell of trees and water,
you beg me to listen and your words enter my spirit.

Your descriptions unmake me; I am like wood
that thought has wormed; even the angels

that report our innermost wish must be kinder.
And yet, when your face is grey in the pillow, I wake you

gently, kissing your eyes, my need for you
stronger than the hope of love. I carry your body

where the hillside flickers: olive cypress ash.
But nothing brings relief. All our days

are numbered in a book. I try to imagine
a way our story can end without a magician.

Lisson Grove

It is hot July, and sycamore wings lodge
in the windscreen wipers. In your illness,
you are begging me to make sense of your life,

and I am helpless as the single electric fan
whirring in the heat of your room
in the Charter Nightingale hospital.

At your bedside, I feel like someone
who has escaped too lightly
from the great hell of the camps,

except that I don't altogether escape,
when I open the door to the street:
the air is cooler, the sky night blue,

but my shoes knock lonely notes from the pavement,
and two tramps salute my return to the car
with ironic cheers and cans of Special Brew.

Separations

There's a whir of wood pigeons this morning:
I should close the study window. Last Spring
two of them tried to build their nest in the music;
big, stubborn birds you had to shift with a broom,
and as the papers fell to the floor I remembered
the scattered papers in that rented room,

when I stayed with you the first time, and how
deeply we overslept, as if in finding each other
our dreams had joined at once in a single stream,
so we could escape the ordinary world, and
make common cause together like comrades
at the end of Clair's *A nous la liberté*.

Ungainly, unworldly creatures we were,
two playing cards precariously leaning
and propping each other up, a friend observed.
But conversation was what you wanted,
some exchange of thought, while I
needed tenderness more than talk.

And so things often went wrong.
We were happy enough exploring the red-light
district in Lille with a lonely Belgian crook, or taking
vodka and pilchards in a house of refuseniks
but at home both of us turned away. You
played music upstairs, I lived in my own song

or on the phone. Now, I've closed the study window.
This morning the sky is pale blue in the birch tree
and you lie asleep, your mouth hurt by last
night's squabble. Will we never escape
the need to sift through the long past together
in our effort to establish a new shape?

Bonds

There are owls in the garden and a dog barking.
After so many fevers and such loss,
I am holding you in my arms tonight, as if
your whole story were happening at once:
the eager child in lonely evacuation
waking into intelligence and then
manhood when we were first *copains*,
setting up tent in a rainy Cornish field, or
hitchhiking down to Marseilles together.

You were braver than I was and so
at your side I was never afraid, looking for
Dom 99 in the snows of suburban Moscow,
or carrying letters through Hungarian customs,
I learnt to trust your intuitions more than my own,
because you could meet Nobel laureates,
tramps and smugglers with the same confidence,
and your hunches worked, those molecular puzzles,
that filled the house with clay and wire models.

In the bad times, when like poor Tom Bowling,
you felt yourself gone for ever more,
and threw away all you deserved, you asked me
What was it all for? And I had no answer, then
or a long time after that madness;
nor can I now suggest new happiness,
or hope of good fortune, other than
staying alive. But I know that lying at your side
I could enter the dark bed of silence like a bride.

Muse

Dissolute, undressed, indoors, we argue
about the old days, how once there was
a time for such pursuits

and how the tender words were spiced
with garlic and rosemary, like
the flesh of a young lamb.

– Is poetry something between
cookery and sacrifice? I murmur
as we pack the goods for market.

– Be quiet. Look. The beech trees are golden,
the air has autumn in it, and the street
lies rain-washed and clean in October sun.

Birdwatching

The birds are returning in May, the curlews and sandpipers,
the kittiwake foraging by the harbour; and two
white headed gulls are setting up together
across the street from our Tromso balcony.
Already they are bonded, they mew to one another;

as one swoops off, the other stretches above the chimney
to look for his return. They caress each other's
plumage with their beaks. We learn they should make
their nest near a lake which this year is still frozen.
Sometimes, we are told, gulls miss the chance to breed,

sometimes they nest in chimneys. We are told the young birds
are clumsy and unruly, learn to fly slowly,
grow larger than parents who remain patient
and bewildered. As the days pass, we grow worried for them.
We take turns watching through binoculars.

In Tromso, seagull eggs, eaten with local beer
are served cut open like an avocado, the thin
shell pale green and mottled. Friends assure us
the gull population rises every year nevertheless.
But I am squeamish about lifting the yolk to my lips.

Picnic

For Roy Tommy Eriksen

Here on the far side of Whale island
where the water is bottleglass blue,
we are having a picnic. There's a dazzle
of sunshine on snow, and around us
mountains cut sharp as crystal.

We are 70 degrees North, but
the landscape is warmed by the drift
of Caribbean waters, and this is
May, the dark time is past
in the Norwegian Arctic.

These are the seas of Greenland halibut,
and catfish with teeth and tongue, yet
it is a gentle Renaissance scholar
who makes a bonfire between stones,
and hangs a kettle on a found stick.

His red-haired wife laughs over
sizzling meat. The sunlight is euphoric.
And on the way home the same friend
ignored a painful back to climb over the edge
of a cliff to rescue your lost denture.

26

After the Arctic

Flew South, still drugged with white sunshine,
dry-skinned, already used to a few streets
between snow slopes, painted wooden
homes, mountains in every window.
We found fresh leaves on birch trees,

damp green of the first chestnut,
yellow blossom, all the tenderness
of English spring. And the next morning
we woke to birdsong, but were ill-tempered,
as if denied an accustomed euphoriant.

Wheelchair

We've travelled on a bumboat on the green South China seas,
seen papaya, dates and coconuts in crotches of the trees
and in Hawker centres Singapore keep quietly policed
eaten hundred year old eggs and fishbrains wrapped in bamboo
    leaf.
We've seen coolies who sold goats milk and the men who
        plundered them
while the ghosts of Maugham and Coward haunt the new Raffles
        hotel;

but the most surprising feature of the perils we have passed
is you've travelled in a wheelchair with your left leg in a cast.
Most people would have had more sense, but we were both
        surprised
to find it rather soothing. And one day we surmised:
you needed an attention that I hardly ever pay
while I enjoyed the knowledge that you couldn't get away.

Now the generator flickers far inland in Campuhan
and we lie inside our cottage cooled remotely by a fan,
or take a bath among the ferns and tall hibiscus trees.
Green rice grows in the paddy fields, we pick the coffee beans.
And outside, parked and ready, sits the chair that takes you round
to explore in a contentment that we've only rarely found.

Dead Writers

In Pushkin's house, it is all as it was
when he went out to duel with d'Anthès:
his wife's elegant needlework, the household bills.

Akhmatova's single room now holds
a golden chair, her oak desk and her bed;
all is tidiness, where once there was disorder.

Russia treasures her poets, once they're dead.
In England, we depend on one another:
the trees my friend planted, grown to a forest,

the white lace bed once offered for my solace.
The river at his garden end flows cold and fast.
Stories, suffering, poetry. All as it was.

The White Bird

For Anna Akhmatova

How marvellously you squandered yourself,
Anna Andreevna, your Tatar bearing
royal in a casual shawl, and wearing
a ring that was a gift of the moon.

Always a witch not a wife, in the house
of three husbands your most
adulterous love was for
the poems they didn't want written

and you could never abandon.
Even as the gay sinner of Tsarskoye Selo,
the future cast its shadow into your heart.
Tonight, I drink to your ruined house,

loneliness, and that white bird
you chose instead of happiness.

Fyodor: Three Lyrics

1

In Bad Homburg, I watched him over the tables,
the homely face, false teeth, poor clothes.
I'm a Swiss doctor, but I read novels.

When he had lost every coin from his worn purse
he looked up at me and smiled:
'I am a man,' he said, 'without a future.'

I had treated him the night before
for epilepsy, and he spoke then of
the joy he felt while lying on the floor

one moment before the foam and spasms.
His face was shining there as he explained:
'Christ alone,' he said, 'can save Russia.'

In Basel, the church floats in the moon
and the trees whiten. There is no casino.
I met him once again with his new wife,

looking at Holbein's coffined Christ,
that decomposing body, green and blue,
the swollen limbs like ripened gooseberries.

He turned, and though he did not recognise
my face, answered my greeting so:
'I shall burn everything I once worshipped.'

What were his sins, then, more than recklessness,
disorder, and a young wife's jewels pawned?
I sometimes wonder if perhaps his genius

(so foreign to this sober, cobbled city
piled above gorges where the black Rhine flows)
had in the very sob of its own pity

another throb of cruelty and pleasure
that made the writing shimmer. Well, I know
I do more human good here as a doctor.

Exile

For Joseph Brodsky

Once you gave me New York.
You led me under a bridge to look
from a wasteland of broken bottle
and beer-can up at the mirror glass
boat of Manhattan. I don't know why
you never went back to your baroque

pale-green city, with the grey Neva
flowing down to the Baltic, but then,
we've not been close, Joseph, though
it happened I was with you when
twenty years ago, you heard
about that first bypass, and so

can remember you talking, as if to yourself,
imagining what it meant to be dead,
with an ironic slant to your face,
and the love of pleasure in your full under-lip
as you nodded up at an untidy bookshelf.
'After that, there is only the book,' you said.

Companionship

It was Wordsworth's clear line I wanted,
nothing to do with mountains, only the quiet
sunshine and silence, but I hated being alone.
The lonely cannot love solitude.

I wanted a garden outside tall windows,
winter sun in leafless branches, a cold spring
with crocus in the grass and the first blossom,
and you at work in the same apartment,

my dearest friend. Today I was watching
a grey squirrel fly in the beech trees when
your words reached into me: 'You know,
a poet isn't much of a companion.'

Wigmore Hall

For Martin

In July heat, beneath the frieze of blue where
golden Apollo stands beneath muse and scribe,
the four musicians have removed their jackets;
and in red braces, silver flute in hand,
you pause to smile, and wipe your misted glasses.

Long ago, when you were at school in
Grantchester Meadows, one speech day
in a hot school hall, your hair too long,
untidy, you came on at eight years old,
after the madrigals to play a folk song,

and the sleepy audience of bored
parents and fellow pupils waiting for
the distribution of prizes, slowly began to attend
and burst into applause when the song ended.
You were surprised, and a shy smile

transformed your face. Let's hope
tonight there's no Apollo to be envious
of these notes singing out in curving line,
as you risk putting yourself to the test
rather than dream 'I might have been' from a desk.

Staking Tomatoes

For Adam

The leaves of four droopy tomato plants
release tobacco harshness, as your fingers
that know their way through Chopin on the piano,
try clumsily to tie these stems to a fence.
Neither of us are natural gardeners.

Long ago in the moonlight of Trumpington
we stayed up feeding roots and spraying
leaf curl in the peach tree. You were gallant,
a poet at ten years old, your smile open,
loyally unheeding my neglect.

There are Belmondo lines of laughter now,
while your two daughters watch with admiration.
But those tomatoes grew red and plump,
as it turns out: undeserved gifts,
like stories from your newly fluent pen.

Birthday

For Joel

My golden-eyed and tender-hearted son,
when you were young, you were too gentle even
to kill a spider in the bath, and when

a terrapin escaped its tank and lived
one stubborn month behind a radiator,
its silly courage touched you into tears.

Being so hurt by other creatures' pain,
you grew up slowly. High on home-made
stilts you stomped between the next-door children

like a giant of whom no one was afraid.
And then you lived in Dalkey where the white houses
dazzle and the morning sky falls into

the long blue puddles left by the sea.
The small birds pecked up prawns, or rose
in flocks, while you observed their beauty.

When you pick up your violin to play
these days, music still makes you happy.
What else you want, you can't be brought to say.

Bed

For a grandchild at six months

The summer garden breathes through my
window, baby Natasha. Untroubled on a pillow,
your eyelids in the rapid movement of dreams, you
learn the scent of my skin and hair,
the body warmth of this bed.

And what I'd wish you to inherit is
the sense of your pretty mother and
your father's brave heart, and grow to relish
the ordinary privilege of daylight
in their house of music and easy laughter.

Now let these words be a loving charm
against the fear of loneliness, and
under a cold moon, you may remember
this bundled duvet as somewhere once
familiar, where you came to no harm.

Amy Levy

Precocious, gifted girl, my nineteenth-century
voice of Xanthippe, I dreamed of you last night,
walking by the willows behind the Wren,
and singing to me of Cambridge and unhappiness.

'Listen, I am the first of my kind, and
not without friends or recognition,
but my name belongs with my family
in Bayswater, where the ghosts

of wealthy Sephardim line the walls,
and there I am alien because I sing.
Here, it is my name that makes me strange.
A hundred years on, is it still the same?'

The First Wriggle

Going to buy milk from the corner shop
on a Tuesday in August with the warm rain
tasting of roses, I suddenly felt an illicit
moment of good fortune: a freedom

in which poems could happen.
It's rather like the grander forms of creation.
Worms on Mars should surprise nobody;
life will form, wherever there's opportunity.

Miracles

After reading Richard Dawkins

Let us consider the dance between fig and wasp,
how the fruit is a flower garden, and the wings
of the female insect are torn off upon entering;
that she lays her eggs in the sweetness of the flesh,
and her grubs bear pollen to fertilise the tree.

You explain that the insect must not use all
the flowers in the fig, or the tree will have no seed,
so there are systems that police her greed,
the simplest, that too many eggs lead the fruit
to drop, so that all her grubs die,

which is an evolution both ruthless and accurate:
the unguided cleverness at work on this planet.

White Flowers

Why should I feel a ripple of apprehension
receiving a gift of white flowers in February,
daisies and carnations, delivered to my door
in florist tissue and white ribbon? It's because
my mother wouldn't have them in the house,
before the Spring solstice. However,

I've put them in a stoneware jar. I'm not
much given to acts of defiance, always had
trouble throwing off superstition:
as a child I counted birds, and believed
in lucky numbers. A necklace
I remember of Russian amber

with stones like lions' teeth had to be worn
even to fetch the post in the worst years;
but I don't hold with my own cowardice
so I display these flowers now without
flamboyance, but with resolution:
a gesture in the name of divine reason.

Rumanian Candle

For all the stench of Bucharest car exhaust
with snow in my lashes and eight year old boys
at my sleeve, who couldn't be chased away,
nagging, *'I love you, pretty lady,*
give me five hundred lei,'

what reached me in my fatigue was a light
in the faces of people who love poetry.
Over frozen white fields, where neglected
villages collapse like broken outhouses,
or in the Hapsburg rococo

of Oradea, where talk slithered uneasily
over the last years of the war
I could make out the same glow:
it was like a candle behind the skin
of their lit faces.

Gorilla

London in August, watching
Hancock repeats. His was a very English
genius: that dingy bedsitter with its floral
fifties prints, the bakelite wireless set;
his putty face miming schoolboy
vanity and gloating. His death saddened
us, but shouldn't have surprised.

What he mocked was the rashness
of unprivileged aspiration, and we laughed
at such a prisoning lack of hope, as if
we were outside the bars looking in
at the great sad figure of a gorilla,
one leather prehensile thumb on
the ball of his jaw. Only we weren't
outside, we were caught in the same system.

Greek Gender

As we learn the new alphabet, a woman is bent
over a pail of paint, white-washing her doorstep.

When we look back along the narrow street, another
woman dressed in black is passing, laden with potatoes.

At the next table, three handsome men in shirtsleeves
sit quietly drinking coffee. We grasp the pronouns,

even the awkward neuters. Above us,
the male tree of a pair of figs is heavy with false fruit.

Holidays

Here on the terrace by the donkey path
we watch old women picking wild spinach.
There are goats to be milked, and cheese to be made.
In Greece, human work has its simplicities.

Holiday makers have to make their own rhythms,
which are not so easy to find: sleep
in the afternoon, swimming in the late sun.
And thinking about the work we left behind.

Visiting Hospital

Walking through so many wards to look for you
surrounded by books and papers, wide awake

and wanting to talk, I pass those other patients
snoring in their beds and must remember

Larkin's old fools and what we shall all find out.
Now I would guess we see only the tether

of sleepers who leave nurses and treatment behind
to dream of their own childhood more often than dying.

Their teeth grin in a glass; their silence breathes.
Even in their depleted lives, they do not feel completed.

Haverstock Hill

It is a cold March day, and
a leafless tree is singing fiercely:
the bird, if there is a bird, invisible,
the voice of mating and territory
rising from dry boughs in vegetable
and ventriloquist urgency.

It is an accident of a shift in the axis
of the turning earth, but I am listening
to life drawn from town soil, and
the radiance of pale sunlight, as if
to a song of wood that has not been
altogether exhausted by winter.

Mother

My mother wore tweed suits and court shoes.
When she came to school, my form teacher
found her a perfect lady and told me henceforth
my wild behaviour wouldn't be excused.

'If you came from a slum it would be different.'
She didn't know her words filled me with glee.
I hated the thought of turning into someone who
carried gloves and couldn't drive a car and I didn't want

to make fine pastry or keep the linen in order.
'Woman,' my father said, 'where is my dinner?'
It was his joke to pretend that mastery
though altogether he depended on her

while she, like her unmarried brother and sister,
could have lived quite cheerfully as a spinster.
I was too afraid of inheriting her colon
cancer and her stoic mildness

to copy her ways, or even to see how
much her tender courage gave to me
a stubborn daughter keeping my own stall
earning a livelihood by telling stories.

Old Movies

At fifteen, in a Torquay cinema
Bacall and Bogart dazed me
with a flash of sexual recognition:
the electricity of their grand adventure
was worth more than a whole comfortable life.

My parents were perplexed.
Years later, I wept in the rain
of a Leicester cemetery and
remembered their quiet happiness.
Now I know: it's love we crave not sex.

Allegiance

We like to eat looking at boats. At night
in Jaffa harbour, the whole sea is alight
with glow worms of the local fisherman's floats.

My English friend has blue flirtatious eyes
and feels no danger. Her intrepid forbears
first explored, then colonized the planet.

Now over Yemenite eggplant and fried dough
we talk about the Roman exploitation
of Caesarea two thousand years ago

and find the history easy to agree.
Politics here and now are another matter.
The scared, open faces of the soldiers

look like oppressors to her, while my inheritance
– Kovno, Odessa, packing and running away –
makes me fear for them, as if they were sons.

So I can't share the privilege of guilt. Nor could
she taste the Hebrew of Adam in
the red earth here: the iron, salt and blood.

Ninety Two

If he was listening he made no sign,
my uncle in his Blundell Sands nursing home.
Under the tight bedclothes I could see
his limbs were skinny as a grasshopper's;
there was even a frictional insect noise
from time to time as he rubbed dry hands together.
I began giving him family news, and was soon apologising
for leaving him up North in his comfortable prison

so I could get on with my own living.
He said nothing, until I mentioned a son
who didn't want to marry, then he murmured
'I never did either' with sudden clarity.
I decided my casual thought was
the first to enter his inner world, because
the rest of my gossip had no relevance

to the story he was moving through.
I was ashamed of my own egotism.
He was engaged once. When that went wrong
he lived alone, played golf, and though
girls liked him, lived a bachelor. 'Was there
no one else then?' I asked him curiously.
In the long pause, I watched him try to remember.

Morden Tower

Went North last week, to read at Morden Tower
after thirty years: do you remember
that 'Stray Dog' of a generation far
from Petersburg, and without Akhmatova,

of Harwood and Raworth, Fisher and Crozier,
Ginsberg on tour, and Basil Bunting?
Behind the same postern door, up
stone steps from Back Stowell Street,

the hipster North waited. I was in something
shiny and Japanese, my long hair loose,
my nerves twitching. Later,
when I crossed two fields in a gale

to the shepherd's hut where Tom Pickard
lived with his red-haired Connie, I was still
too scared to eat their sorrel soup. They saw me
as someone from the squeamish South,

but I was no more comfortable in Cambridge
than I am now a part of the new age.
Poets don't fit. Never have. I guess
we'll just have to trust the words on the page.

Rosemary in Provence

We stopped the Citroen at the turn of the lane,
because you wanted a sprig of blue rosemary
to take home, and your coat opened awkwardly

as you bent over. Any stranger would have
seen your frail shoulders, the illness
in your skin – our holiday on the Luberon

ending with salmonella –
but what hurt me, as you chose slowly,
was the delicacy of your gesture:

the curious child, loving blossom
and mosses, still eager
in your disguise as an old man.

Party Time

It's lovely in the bathroom:
green marble floor, cool tiles
and trailing plants. Sometimes
I can't think why anybody wants
to plod around a room explaining
who they are and what they care about.
In here I am quite happy alone
with my own thought.

After a time, though, and long before
that urgent knock on the door, I remember
how, when things have gone most
seriously wrong, a group of people
no more intimate than this
have sometimes had the power to restore
a sense of who I am. It's lovely
in the bathroom nevertheless:
but not for long.

Mirror

Mirror, mirror, what's going on?
A matron aunt or stubborn father
these days looks out of the mirror.
When I smile at them they are gone.

A pace behind the silvered glass
they wait like ghosts, though not so much
scary as shy, eager to touch
my present flesh with their own past.

Within my body is a thread
of which resemblance is the sign:
my story is not only mine
but an extension of the dead.

Prayer

The windows are black tonight. The lamp
at my bedside peering with its yellow
40 watt light can hardly make out the chair.
Nothing is stranger than the habit of prayer.

The face of God as seen on this planet
is rarely gentle: the young gazelle is food
for the predator; filmy shapes
that need little more than carbon and water,

evolve like patterns on Dawkins'
computer; the intricate miracles
of eye and wing respond to the same
logic. I accept the evidence.

God is the wish to live. Everywhere,
as carnivores lick their young with
tenderness, in the human struggle
nothing is stranger than the habit of prayer.